A Big Bat

by Lada Josefa Kratky

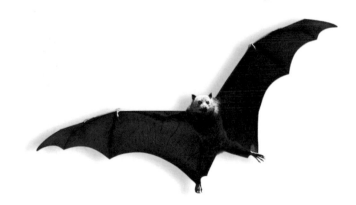

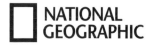

NATIONAL
GEOGRAPHIC

School Publishing

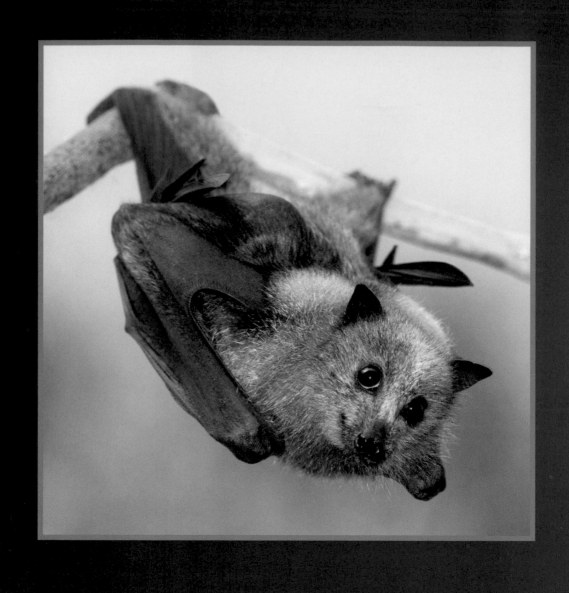

This is a bat.

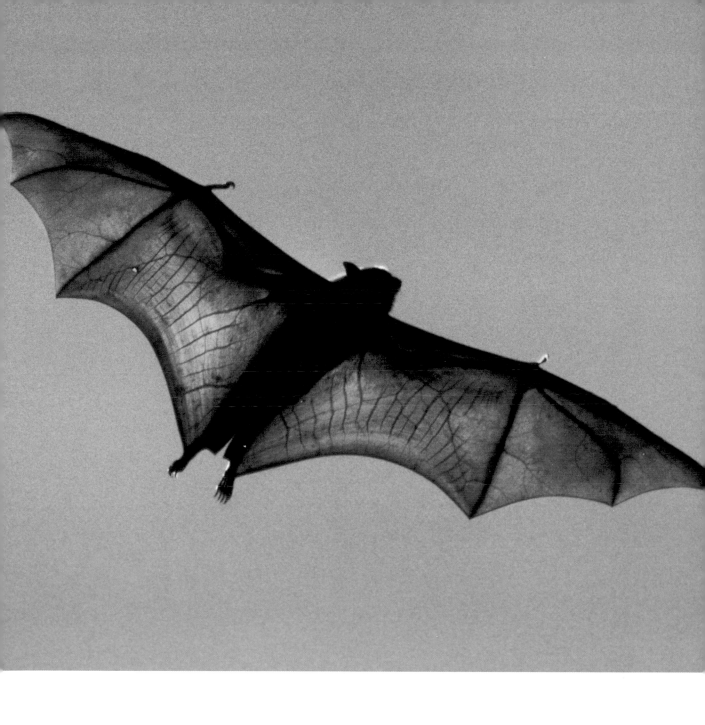

This bat is big.

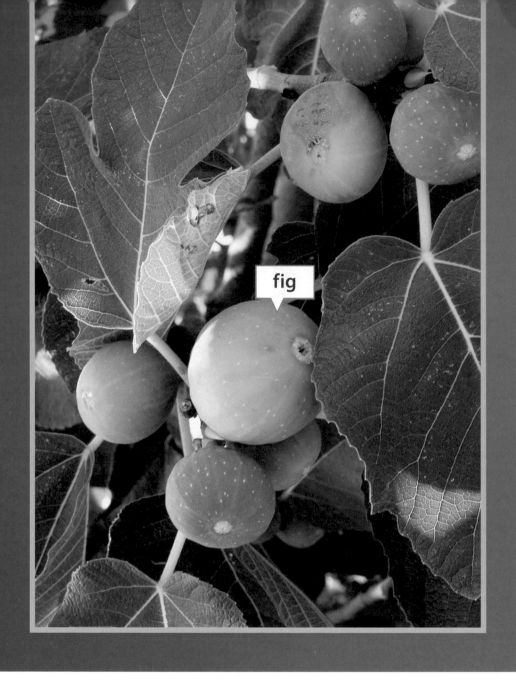

fig

Look, a fig!

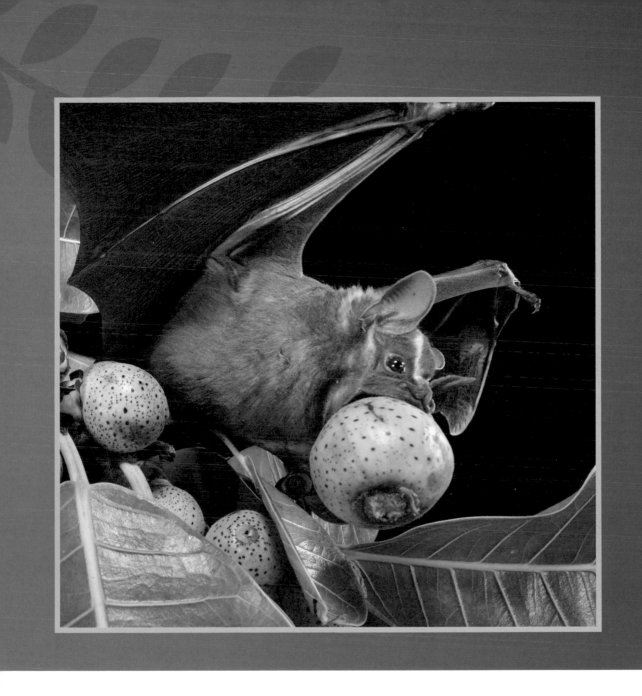

The bat bit the fig.

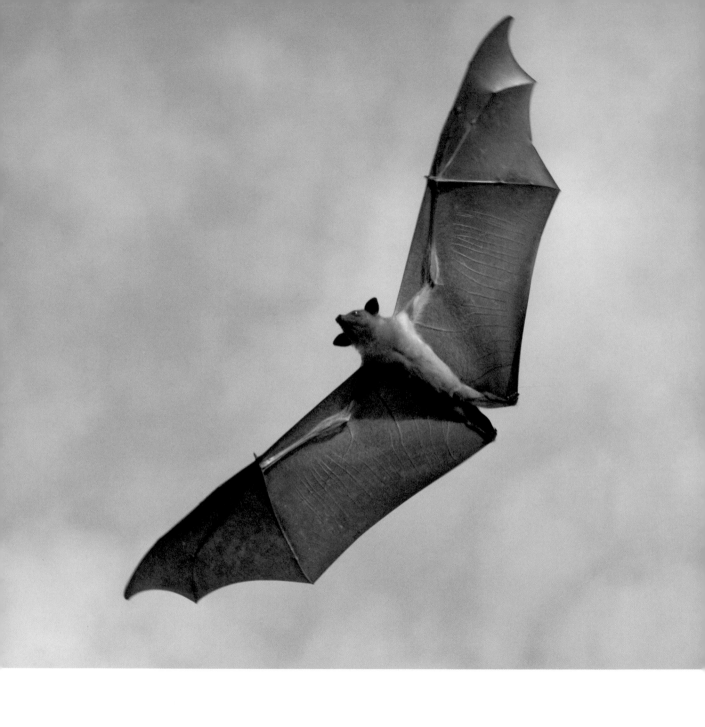

This bat can go fast.

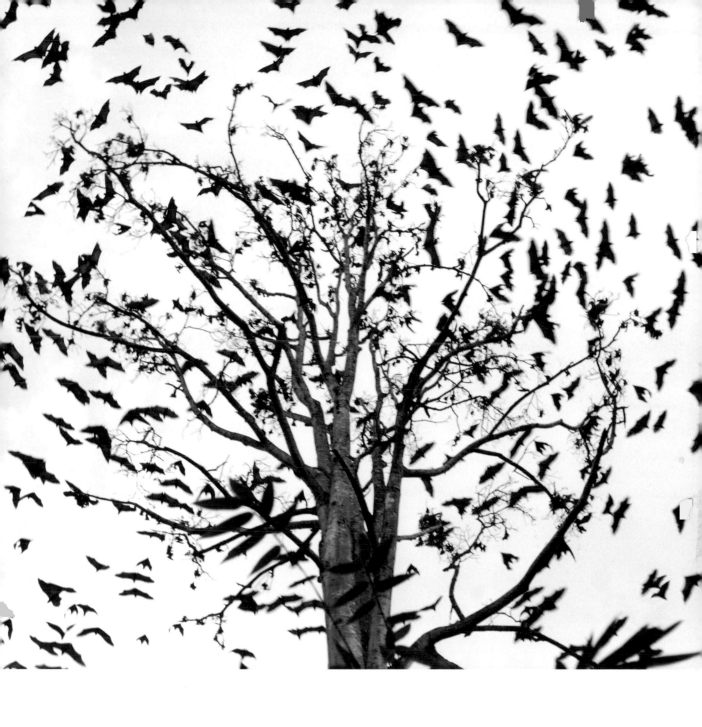

Go, bats, go!

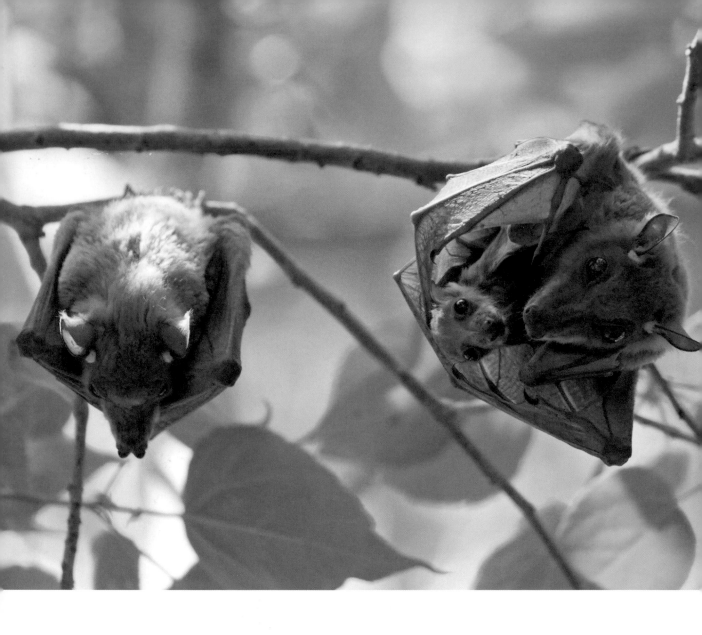

Can this bat nap?
Yes, it can!